FIRST SCIENCE

written by Jillian Harker

designed and illustrated by Claire James

Ladybird Books

Home sweet home!

Home is the place we know best.
How much do you know about
your home?

Look at these things around your house.
Are they made of wood? Write **w**
plastic? Write **p**
metal? Write **m**

w

p

p

w

Home and dry

Try this experiment to find out about the walls of houses.
Colour the two sugar walls to show what happens.

food colour +water

sugar cubes

food colour +water

dishes

strip from plastic bag

The same thing happens with bricks.
Why do house walls have a damp-proof layer?

Tick here if you can find the
damp-proof layer in your house.

BUILD A HOUSE: Use wax crayons and thin strong paper to make
rubbings from outside walls, paths and other surfaces near your
house. Hold the paper in place with Blu-tack.™ Cut the rubbings
into brick shapes and make a collage of a house.

Close to the wind

How draughty is your house?
Make a draught checker.

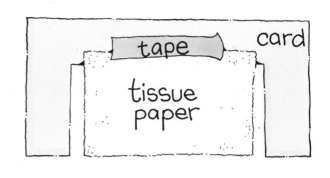

Hold your checker against the
sides, bottom and top of the
doors and windows.
Put **X** on the pictures to show where the draught moved the
tissue paper.

Try other places.
How many draughty places did you find?

Are you switched on?

Which of these use electricity in *your* home?
Write ∧∧∧

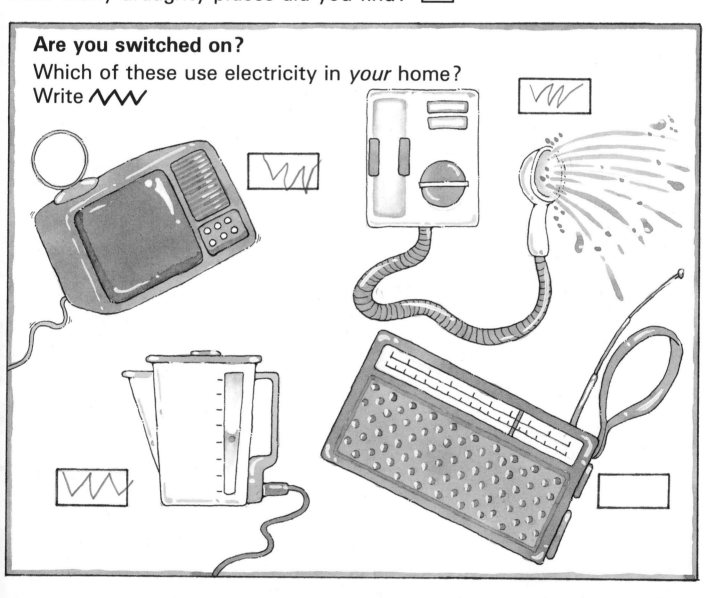

In the kitchen...

You can be a scientist in your own kitchen.
Let's see what you can find out.

① Use an empty washing-up liquid bottle.

② make a row of holes and cover with sticky tape

③ fill bottle with water

④ Remove the tape. On this picture draw what you see happen.

Tick the correct boxes.

The longest spray came from the   top ☐ hole.

middle ☐

bottom ☐

There is more force (**pressure**) from   a little ☐   water.

a lot of ☐

SPRAY AWAY: How far can you squirt water from a washing-up liquid bottle? Try it in the garden. Change the slope of the bottle. Which slope gives the longest squirt?

Sink or swim

Put a ball of Plasticine and a sieve in warm water.
Now see if you can make them float.

Clues: Try changing the shape of one thing. Try using cling film or a plastic bag.

Write ∗ in the box.

I made the Plasticine float ☐

I made the sieve float ☐

Using hot air

When air is heated it swells (**expands**).
Hot air can make things move.
See this yourself by trying an experiment.
Squeeze the air out of a plastic bottle.
Put the top back on.
Stand the bottle in hot water.
Wait and watch.
Now stand the bottle in cold water. Wait and watch.

Replace the top

  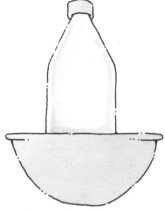

HOT
COLD

Draw a line from each word to the correct picture.

Watercolours

Which colours are mixed together to make your felt-tips?

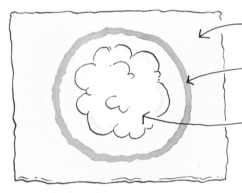

blotting paper

black felt-tip circle

wet cotton wool

Try black, brown and green felt-tips.
Finish the sentence by colouring the boxes.

was made from ☐☐☐ ...
was made from ☐☐☐ ...
was made from ☐☐☐ ...

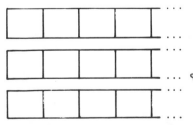

BUTTERFLIES: Cut butterfly shapes from blotting paper.
Draw circles in felt-tip on the wings. Now use wet cotton wool
to turn the circles into beautiful wing patterns.

Everyday things...

Each day we use all sorts of things without really thinking about them. Let's see if we can discover something new.

Link with a line any *two* things which could be made of the same material.

Which of these are made from something which was once alive? Circle the pictures.

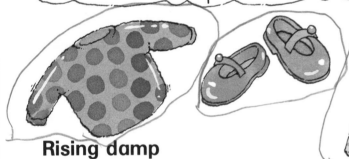

Rising damp

Which of these strips of paper soaks up (**absorbs**) water?

When something does not absorb water we say it is **waterproof**. Test some food wrappings to see if they are waterproof.

plain paper
glass
2cm of water

paper covered with wax crayon
glass
2cm of water

Write **w** for waterproof.
Write **a** for absorbent.

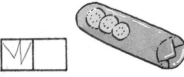

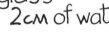

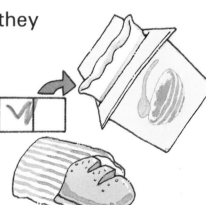

Now tick the second box if you think the food will keep fresh for a long time.

MORE RUBBINGS: Make the same rubbings as you made for Home sweet home, this time using white wax crayon or a white candle. Paint over them with **thin** paint. How are they different from your first patterns?

A magnet in the fridge

Open your fridge door.
Can you see a lock or a catch?

Tick: Yes ☐   No ☑

Why does the door stay closed?

Try sticking
a paper clip
to the rubber
round the
fridge door.

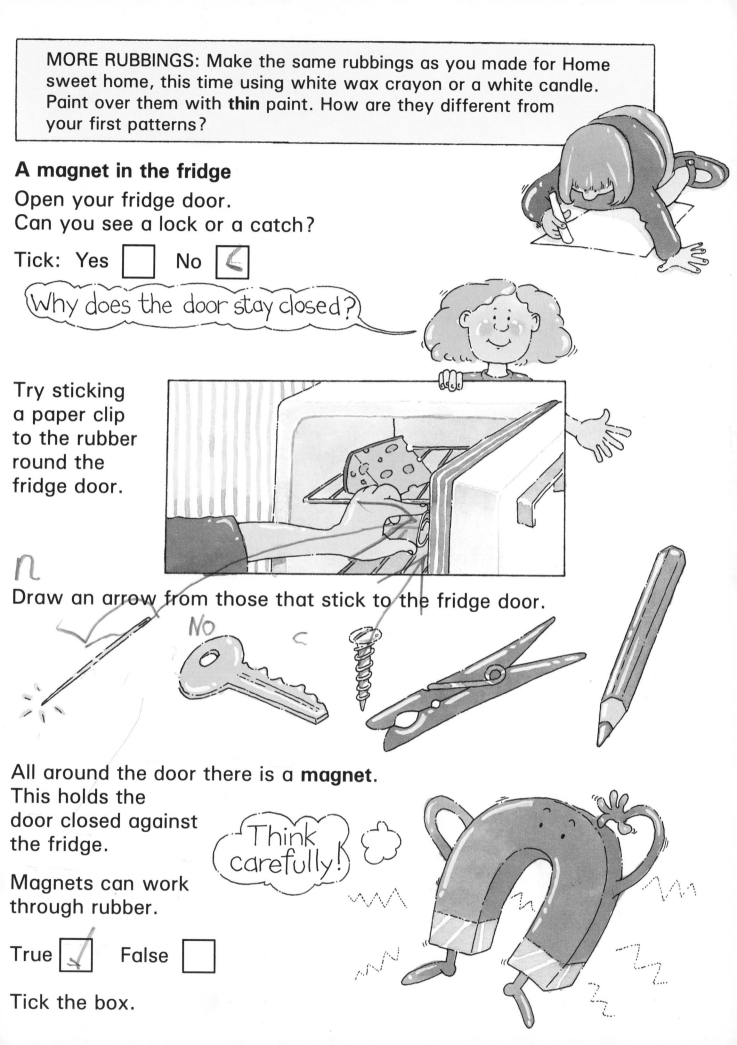

Draw an arrow from those that stick to the fridge door.

All around the door there is a **magnet**.
This holds the
door closed against
the fridge.

Think carefully!

Magnets can work
through rubber.

True ☑   False ☐

Tick the box.

Playing around

Toys and games can teach us a lot about science.
Here are some ideas for you to try.

Which toys use air in some way?
Circle the pictures.

Ups and downs

Take a ball.
Drop it onto a path –

←from this height

←from this height

←from this height

Count how many times it bounces.
Fill in the chart. Put ⌒ for each bounce.
Try again, dropping the ball onto grass.

Path

knee	waist	shoulder

Grass

	3	
2	2	34
knee	waist	shoulder

Which surface gave the most bounces?
Write ≋ in the box.   Path ☐   Grass ☐

Which wall is stronger?

Make two walls from interlocking bricks.
Like these:

Test the walls by swinging a Plasticine ball against each one.
Both walls will fall over.
Draw a ring round the wall which did **not** fall to pieces.

Wheels

How many different toys do you have
with wheels?

Write the number.

Experiment with wheels that you can make from card.

Which wheels ran most smoothly? Write ✳

Which wheels ran quite smoothly? Write ?

Which wheels ran bumpily?　　　　Write ⌒

The ground beneath our feet

Have you ever really thought about the ground you walk on?
Let's look more closely. Try this:

newspaper
trowel
soil

Did you find any of these in the soil?
Tick the boxes.

What is soil made of?

add water

soil

Let the soil settle. Now draw in this jar what you see
in your own jar. Use the pictures below to help you.

big pieces
smaller pieces
sand
twigs and leaves
water

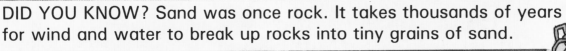

A slippery character?

Dig up a worm.
Can you hear it move?

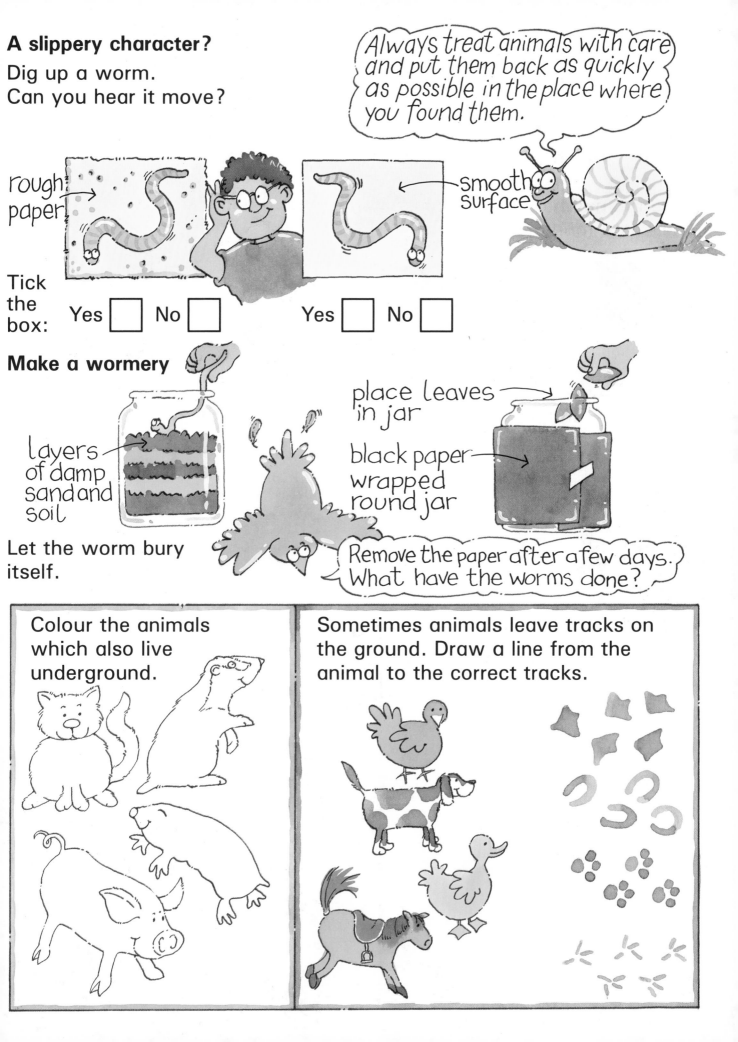

Always treat animals with care and put them back as quickly as possible in the place where you found them.

rough paper

smooth surface

Tick the box:

Yes ☐ No ☐   Yes ☐ No ☐

Make a wormery

place leaves in jar

layers of damp sand and soil

black paper wrapped round jar

Let the worm bury itself.

Remove the paper after a few days. What have the worms done?

Colour the animals which also live underground.

Sometimes animals leave tracks on the ground. Draw a line from the animal to the correct tracks.

Millions of minibeasts...

There is plenty of wildlife to be found in even the smallest of gardens. Which of these can you find in *your* garden?

Write the number of the minibeast in one of the circles to show where you found it.

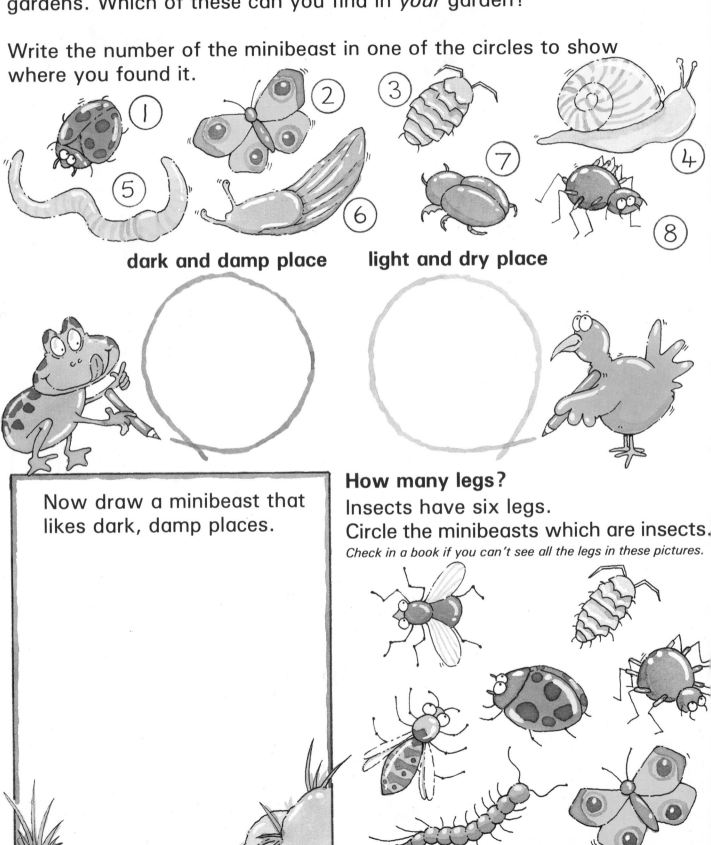

dark and damp place

light and dry place

Now draw a minibeast that likes dark, damp places.

How many legs?
Insects have six legs.
Circle the minibeasts which are insects.
Check in a book if you can't see all the legs in these pictures.

Come to the circus!

On the moon...

Make a minibeast

lower half of egg carton

cut here

tissue paper

tissue paper wings

Decorate both halves, sandwich tissue wings between, hold together with two elastic bands

elastic bands

pipe cleaners threaded through middle section

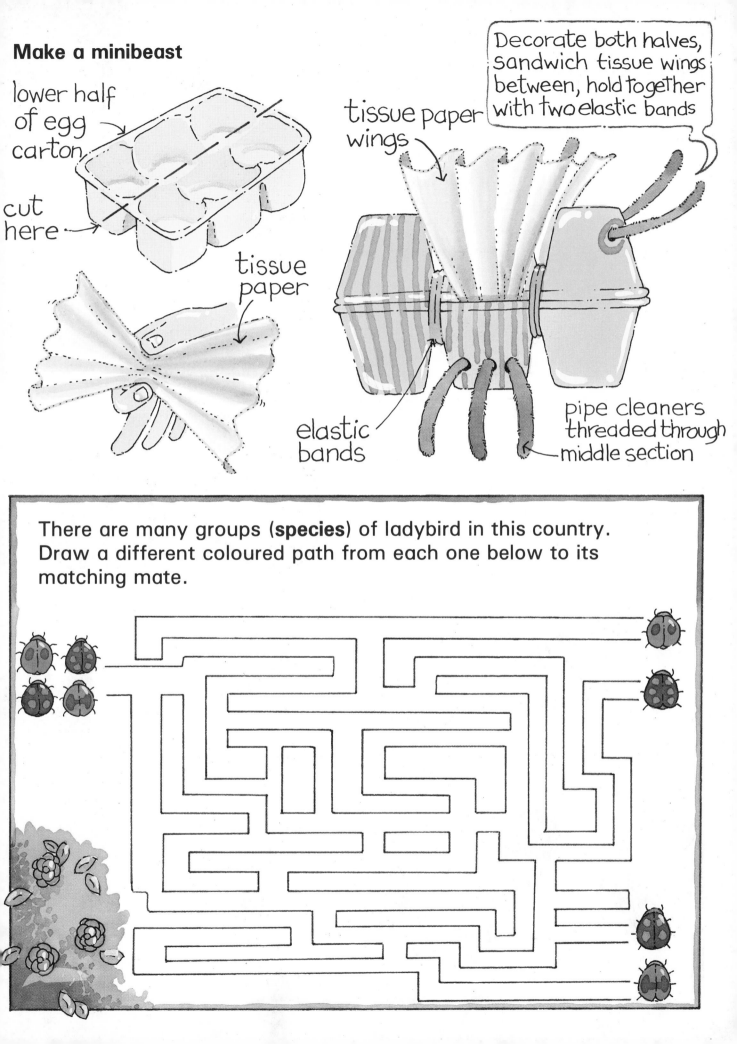

There are many groups (**species**) of ladybird in this country. Draw a different coloured path from each one below to its matching mate.

Reaching for the sky...

Find a tree near your home. What can you find out by looking at it and touching it?
Tell someone all the things you noticed.

Make a foil leaf picture

tin foil

back of leaf

Rub firmly!

cotton wool

Try different leaves. Which one makes the best rubbing?

A tree adds a new **growth ring** round its trunk each year.
We can see these when the tree is chopped down. Count the rings to see how old these trees were.

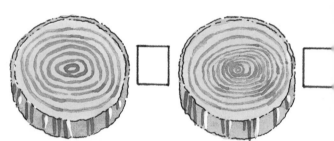

Draw a line from each picture to the correct season.

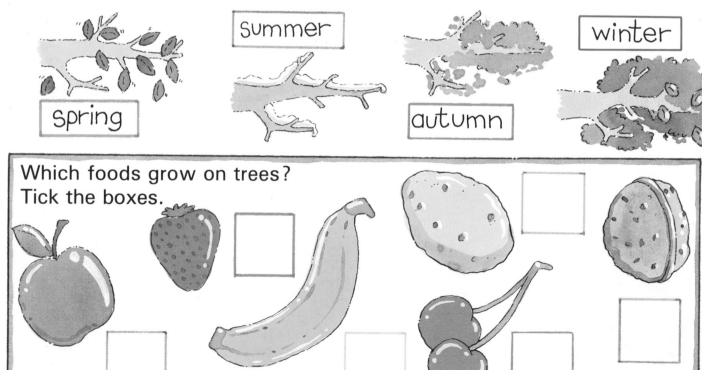

spring

summer

autumn

winter

Which foods grow on trees?
Tick the boxes.

Make a bird feeder

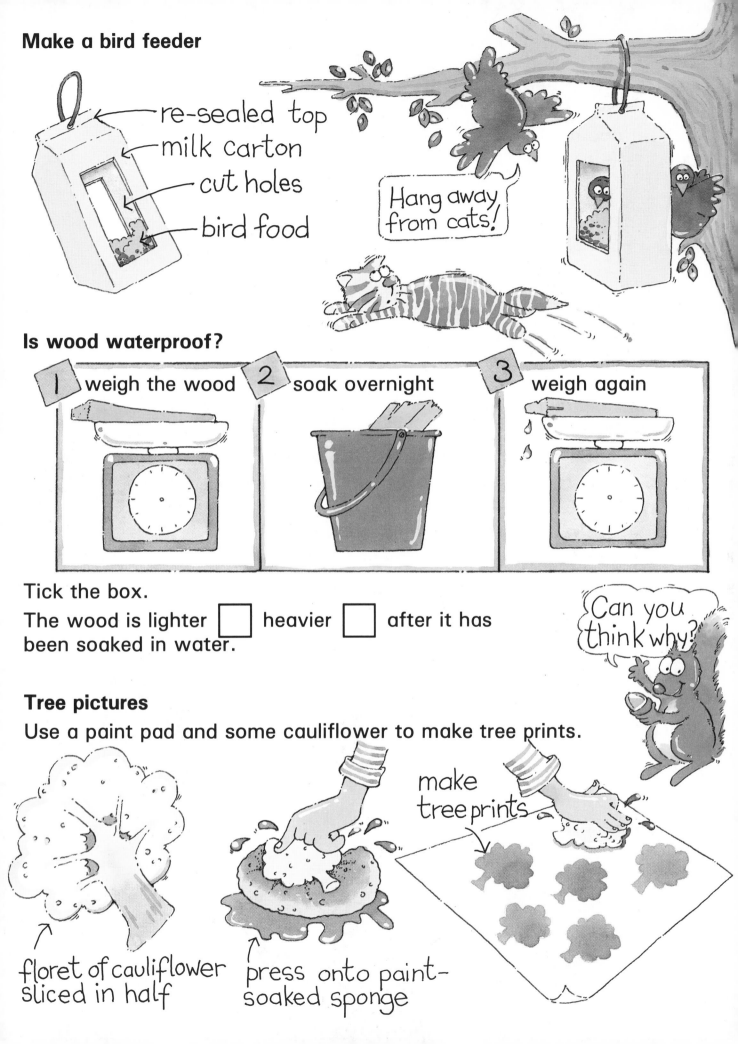

re-sealed top
milk carton
cut holes
bird food

Hang away from cats!

Is wood waterproof?

1 weigh the wood   2 soak overnight   3 weigh again

Tick the box.

The wood is lighter ☐ heavier ☐ after it has been soaked in water.

Can you think why?

Tree pictures

Use a paint pad and some cauliflower to make tree prints.

make tree prints

floret of cauliflower sliced in half   press onto paint-soaked sponge

Bridges and other supports...

Find out about supports (structures).

> Use coins (or building blocks) of equal size as weights.

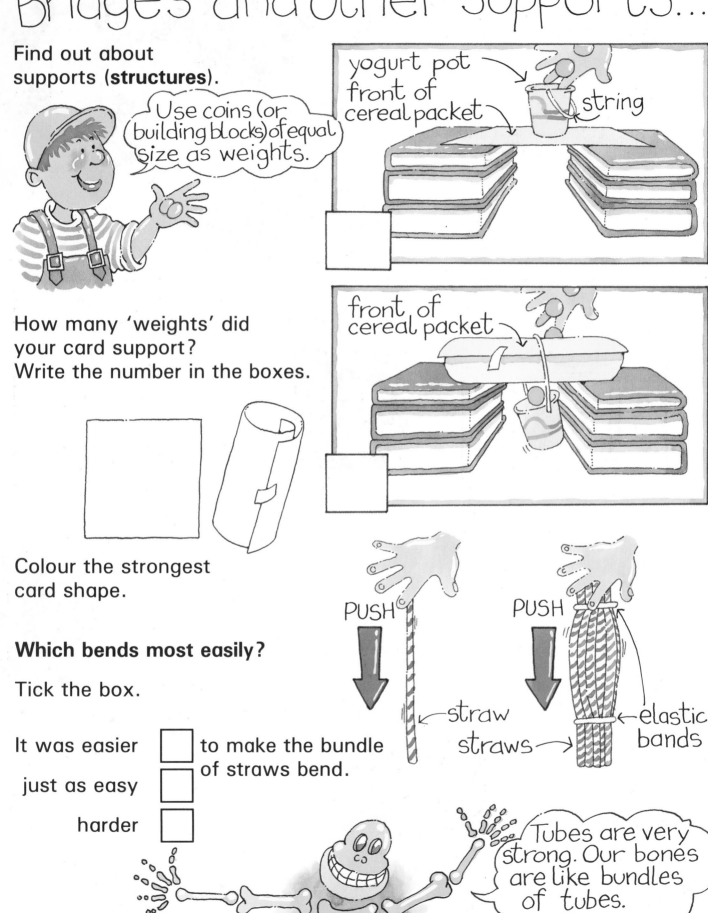

yogurt pot
front of cereal packet
string

front of cereal packet

How many 'weights' did your card support?

Write the number in the boxes.

Colour the strongest card shape.

Which bends most easily?

Tick the box.

It was easier ☐ to make the bundle of straws bend.

just as easy ☐

harder ☐

PUSH
straw

PUSH
straws
elastic bands

> Tubes are very strong. Our bones are like bundles of tubes.

A strong support

Are there other ways to make
structures strong?
Let's try to find out.
Use the same piece of card
in different
ways.

front of
cereal packet

back of
cereal packet

folded
front of
cereal packet

How many weights? Write the number in the boxes.

Cut through the side of a thick cardboard box.
Draw what you see between the outside layers of card.

_____

_____

Make sure the legs are
straight.

Tall and short

The position of supports can be very important.
Make two Plasticine animals of the same size
and shape.

Give one short legs and the other long legs.

Colour the animal which falls over.

Change the position of the legs on that animal.
When it stands firm, draw it here to show how its legs look.

The way we see it...

Most people depend on their eyes to help them to learn about the world. Circle the things which help us to see more clearly.

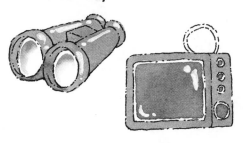

Make a magnifying glass

Tick the box.

Through the drop of water the print looked smaller. ☐

the same ☐

larger ☐

sheet of plastic on top of paper

drop of water

newspaper

Eyes front!

Eyes are very important for many animals.

Which of these animals are hunters (**predators**)? Write **h**

Which are food (**prey**) for others? Write **f**

Clue: Hunters often have their eyes on the front of their head. Prey need their eyes on the side of their head to keep a look out for danger.

☐ ☐ ☐ ☐ ☐

DID YOU KNOW? A dragonfly has 30,000 sides (**facets**) in its eye which give it excellent all-round sight.

Can our eyes play tricks on us?

A picture (**image**) stays 'printed' on our eye for a little while after we have looked at something.

Try these experiments to see how this works.

Stare hard at the red shape. Then move your eyes down and stare hard at the blank space below. Do the same with the green shape.

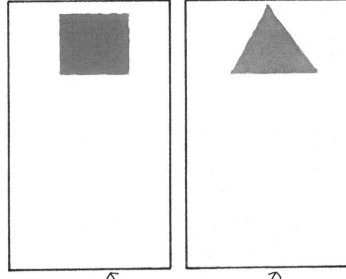

Draw what you see here

Make a spinner

1 Fold a 10 cm paper circle 4 times to divide it into 16 segments.

2 Colour every other segment red and glue your circle to card.

3 Cut out and push a short pencil, point down, through the centre. Spin the disc quickly.

4 Colour this picture to show what you see.

Blind spot

Cover one eye at a time and read the list of numbers. Follow the direction of the arrow. If the spot disappears, put a ring round the numbers where you could not still see the spot.

⇨ • 1 2 3 4 5 6 7 8 9 10 11 12 13 14 15 ☐

Now try in this direction.

1 2 3 4 5 6 7 8 9 10 11 12 13 14 15 • ⇦ ☐

In the box write 'l' for left or 'r' for right to show which eye had the blind spot.

All systems go...

Things move because there is some sort of **force** pushing or pulling them.

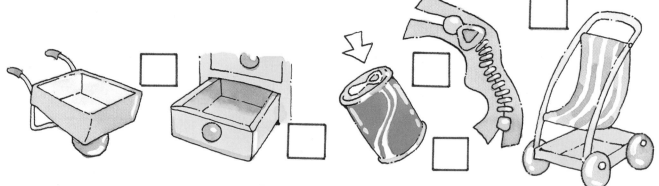

Which of these do we push? Put a tick.
Which do we pull? Put a cross.

Pushing and pulling

We can use the push or pull of one thing to make another move.

Ask for help to remove the coloured bases from two soft drink bottles. The glue melts when soaked in hot water.

Set up the bases as shown. Turn the right-hand base in a clockwise direction.

Draw an arrow to show which way the other one moves.

Now put on the elastic band like this.

Which way does the left base move? Draw an arrow.

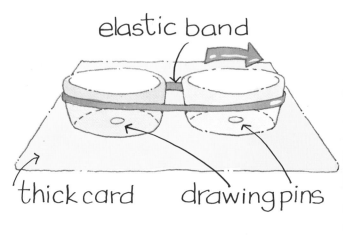

elastic band

thick card   drawing pins

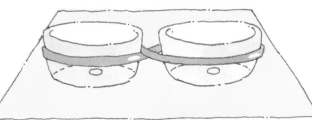

Your body

Bodies are like machines.

Muscles pull different parts of the body to make them move.

Join pairs of animals with a line to show that they move about in the same way.

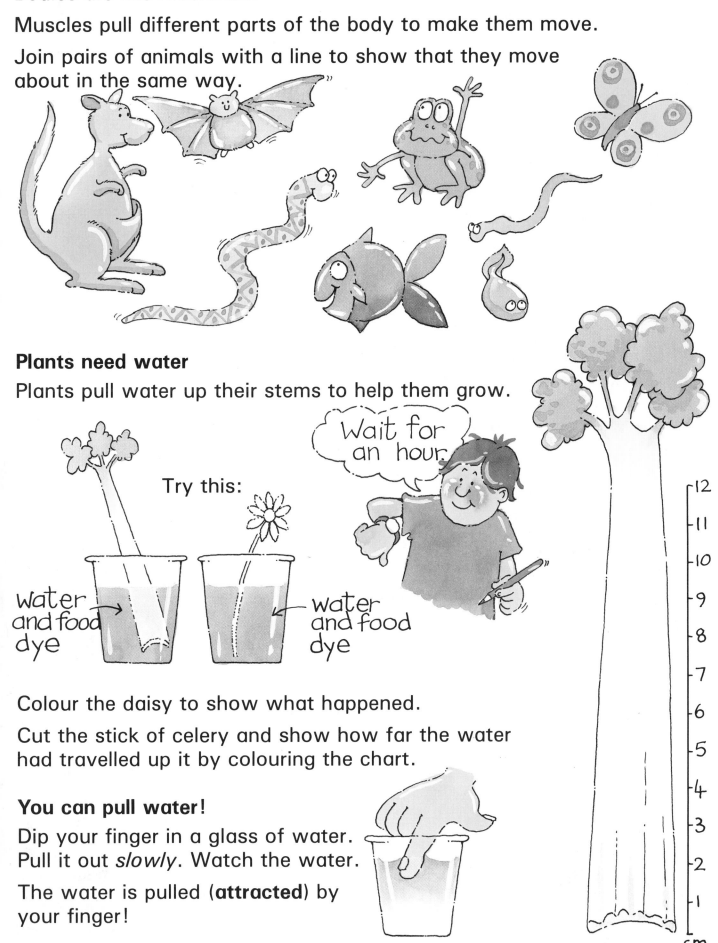

Plants need water

Plants pull water up their stems to help them grow.

Try this:

Wait for an hour.

water and food dye

water and food dye

Colour the daisy to show what happened.

Cut the stick of celery and show how far the water had travelled up it by colouring the chart.

You can pull water!

Dip your finger in a glass of water. Pull it out *slowly*. Watch the water.

The water is pulled (**attracted**) by your finger!

12
11
10
9
8
7
6
5
4
3
2
1

cm

Stop, look and listen...

How well do you use your eyes and ears?

Can you work out the pattern of traffic lights?
Colour the lights to show the pattern.

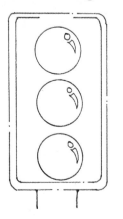 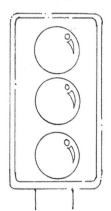 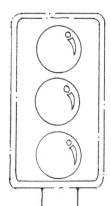 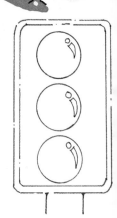

What colour is a candle flame?

Colour the flame below to show what you think it looks like.

Ask for help to light a candle and watch the flame carefully.

Now colour this
flame to show
what you saw.

Be careful

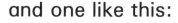

DID YOU KNOW? The peregrine falcon has such good eyesight that
it can spot its prey from a height of 300 metres.

Have you ever noticed the patterns in an apple?

Cut one apple like this:　　　and one like this:

 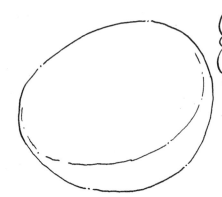

Try other
fruit and
vegetables!

Draw and colour what you see.

Can you hear a watch tick when it's not beside your ear?
Try these experiments.

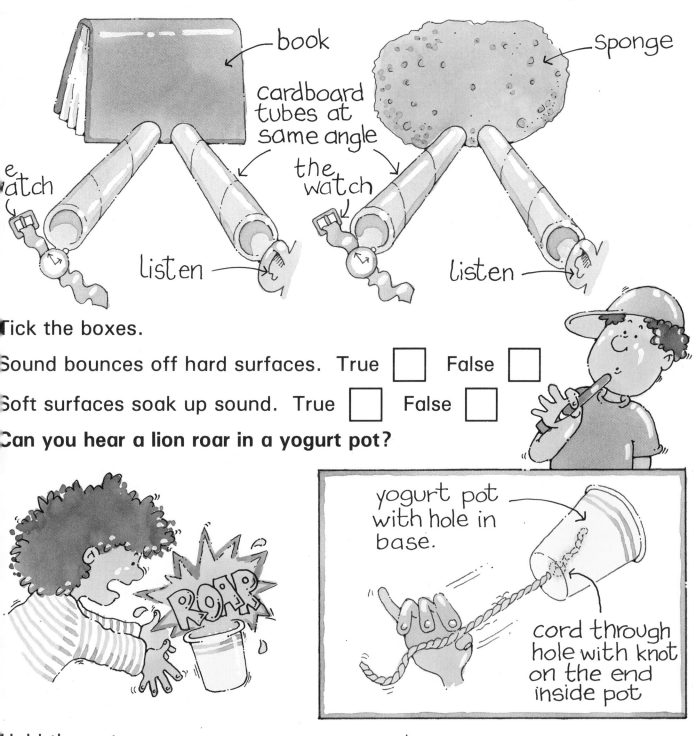

book

cardboard tubes at same angle

sponge

watch

the watch

listen

listen

Tick the boxes.

Sound bounces off hard surfaces. True ☐ False ☐

Soft surfaces soak up sound. True ☐ False ☐

Can you hear a lion roar in a yogurt pot?

ROAR

yogurt pot with hole in base.

cord through hole with knot on the end inside pot

Hold the pot near your ear.
Start near the pot and drag your thumb and finger nail quickly down the cord.
Use your finger tips only to make the lion snore.

DID YOU KNOW? The barn owl can hear so well that it can work out exactly where its prey is, even on the darkest night.

Give yourself a test...

1. When something does not soak up water we say it is water_____.

2. Colour the animal which lives underground.

3. Write in the correct number.
Insects have _____ legs.

4. What do you count to tell the age of a tree?
Tick the answer.

5. Join the words which mean the same.

food

hunter

predator

prey

6. Which colour or colours come next in the traffic light pattern.

7. When air is heated it **expands**.
TRUE ☐   FALSE ☐